LOST AND FOUND

TUTANKHAMUN
AND OTHER
Lost Tombs

JOHN MALAM

QEB Publishing

Copyright © QEB Publishing, Inc. 2011

Published in the United States by
QEB Publishing, Inc.
3 Wrigley, Suite A
Irvine, CA 92618

www.qed-publishing.co.uk

ISBN 978 1 60992 053 1

Printed in the United States

Project Editor Carey Scott
Designer Stefan Morris Design
Illustrations The Art Agency
and MW Digital Graphics
Picture Researcher Maria Joannou

Front cover image: Tutankhamun's death mask,
which was placed over his mummy

Library of Congress Cataloging-in-Publication Data
Malam, John, 1957-
  Tutankhamun and other lost tombs / John Malam.
      p. cm. -- (Lost and found)
  Summary: "Describes the historical circumstances that led to the deaths of and tombs
being built for royalty such as Tutankhamun of Egypt, King Phillip II of Macedonia and
Prince Liu Sheng of China plus the archaeological discoveries that found evidence of and
preserved these tombs"--Provided by publisher.
  Includes index.
  ISBN 978-1-60992-053-1 (library bound)
  1. Tombs--Juvenile literature. 2. Excavations (Archaeology)-Juvenile literature. 3.
Civilization, Ancient--Juvenile literature. I. Title.
  CC77.B8M35 2012
  930.1--dc22
                                                                        2011012123

Picture credits
Key: t=top, b=bottom, r=right, l=left, c=center
Alamy Images Ancient Art & Architecture Collection Ltd 5tl, Steve Davey Photography 9b; **The
Art Agency** Ian Jackson 10bl, 14b, 19, 23b, 27b; **Bridgeman Art Library** Giraudon 25r, Iraq
Museum, Baghdad 29b; **Corbis** Enrique Castro-Mendivil/Reuters 3, Robert Harding World
Imagery 6bl, Sandro Vannini 7t, 8b, Gianni Dagli Orti 10br, The Gallery Collection 13t, Nathan
Benn 15t, Enrique Castro-Mendivil/Reuters 17t, 17b, The Gallery Collection 18b, Fine Art 20t,
Bettmann 27t, Enrique Castro-Mendivil/Reuters 30, Sandro Vannini 32; **Getty Images** Gallo
Images/Mike Copeland 5tr, Hulton Archive 8t, Stone/Michael Melford 9t, National Geographic/
Martha Cooper 16, Hulton Archive 31; **The Manchester Museum** The University of Manchester 13b;
Photolibrary/Barbara Heller 2br, Mario Verin 15b, Barbara Heller 23t, De Agostini Editore 26b; **The Picture
Desk** Art Archive/Archaeological Museum Volos/Gianni Dagli Orti 5b, Art Archive/Genius of China Exhibition
24, Art Archive/Kharbine-Tapabor/Coll. Bouquig. 29t; **Press Association Images** AP Photo 12; **Rex Features**
Sipa Press 1, Brian Harris 21b; **Shutterstock** Dudarev Mikhail 4, Bragin Alexey 2l I.T 7b; **Topham Picturepoint**
2tr, 20b, 28, Luisa Ricciarini 11t, Alinari 11b, Museum of London 19tl, The Granger Collection 21t, 22b,
FotoWare FotoStation 25l. All maps by Mark Walker at **MW Digital Graphics** 6t, 10t, 14t, 18t, 22t, 26t

The words in **bold** are explained in the Glossary on page 31.

10 9 8 7 6 5 4 3 2

CONTENTS

WHAT IS A LOST TOMB?

A tomb is a home for the remains of a dead person—their final resting place on Earth. Tombs can be built above the ground for all to see, buried out of sight under the ground, or cut deep into the rocky side of a mountain or a valley.

Tombs are built by the living to honor the dead. Usually, the more important the dead person, the grander and more sumptuous is the tomb. For ancient people, tombs were the place where the dead person began their life after death. So they were filled with objects for the person to use in the afterlife. These objects might be valuable treasure. The tombs of some kings, emperors, and other rulers even contained the bodies of ordinary people. They were the servants of the ruler and were **sacrificed**—deliberately killed—so they could continue to serve and protect their leader in the afterlife.

▼ The pyramids of Ancient Egypt were built as tombs for the first **pharaohs** (kings). Unfortunately, **tomb robbers** raided every pyramid, and the Ancient Egyptians had to find a safer place to bury their dead kings.

◄ In Ancient Egypt, the **mummified** organs of dead people were kept in their tomb inside containers called canopic jars. Each canopic jar was decorated with a human or animal head.

▲ Burial mounds are tombs that were built in prehistoric times in Europe. Some are simple mounds of earth. Others, such as this one, have passageways leading to a central chamber where the bodies were placed.

As time passes, people stop visiting tombs. Memories fade, and the identities of the dead people buried inside them are forgotten. Eventually, they become lost tombs. Only if they are found by **treasure hunters** or **archeologists,** or by accident, can their hidden treasures be brought back into the world of the living, hundreds or even thousands of years later.

Grave Goods

This is the grave of an ordinary person, containing a few cooking pots for him or her to use in the afterlife. The tombs of important people have contained thousands of objects. These include everyday household goods and food, but also luxury and valuable items, even chariots and ships! But even simple grave goods, such as these, can tell experts something about the person who died and the society they came from.

LOST:
EGYPTIAN PHARAOH

His name was Tutankhamun, and he was the boy king of Ancient Egypt. He became pharaoh when he was just nine years old, and from then on people treated him as a living god. But Tutankhamun's reign was short, because he died when he was about 19 years old.

Location: Valley of the Kings, Egypt
Date: about 1323 BCE

▶ In this painting Tutankhamun is shown in his chariot, firing arrows at his enemies, in one of the wars of Ancient Egypt.

No one expected the king to die so young, and his royal tomb was not yet ready for him. Instead of a fabulous burial place fit for a king, Tutankhamun was given a small tomb intended for an ordinary person. It had four rooms, which were cut into the rock in the side of a valley.

Royal servants mummified Tutankhamun's body to preserve it, and placed a gold mask over his head and shoulders. Then they put the mummy in a nest of three coffins, one inside the other, and lowered these into a stone coffin called a **sarcophagus**. The servants built golden **shrines** around the sarcophagus, until these filled the tomb's burial chamber. They piled the other chambers high with thousands of objects for the king to use in the afterlife. They sealed the door to the tomb, and covered the steps leading down to it from the hillside so that it was completely hidden.

◀ This gold figure of Tutankhamun shows the king wearing a crown of Egypt and holding a crook and flail—symbols of the Egyptian pharaohs.

About 200 years after Tutankhamun was buried, a new tomb was dug into the rock above. It was the tomb of the new pharaoh, Ramesses VI. As the builders tunneled into the cliff, they sent showers of rock tumbling down the cliff. The rocks settled on the ground over Tutankhamun's tomb, burying it even deeper and making it harder for robbers to find. Eventually, his tomb was forgotten, and the boy king was left to rest in peace.

Valley of the Kings

The valley where Tutankhamun was buried is known as the Valley of the Kings. Over about 500 years, more than 60 tombs for pharaohs and nobles were dug there. Some were built deep into the cliffs and had many rooms, but others, such as Tutankhamun's, were much smaller. The tombs were intended to be safe from tomb robbers, but one by one they were broken into and looted. Even Tutankhamun's tomb was raided but the robbers did not find all the treasure. The tomb was closed again, and the robbers never went back.

FOUND: TUTANKHAMUN'S TOMB

The tombs in the Valley of the Kings were robbed in ancient times, and archeologists could only wonder what treasures they had once held. But there was one archeologist who believed there was a lost tomb somewhere in the valley, untouched by robbers and still full of treasures.

▲ Howard Carter carefully removes a layer of hard black pitch—a sticky resin —which covered Tutankhamun's mummy inside the innermost coffin.

▼ This necklace was found on Tutankhamun's mummy. It shows scarab beetles with disks, which represent the Sun and Moon, above their heads.

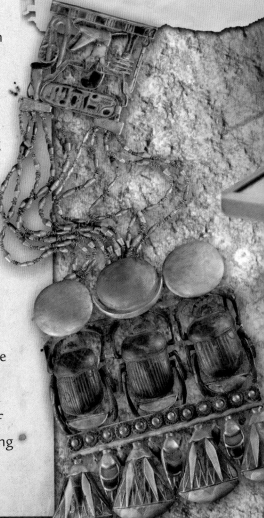

Howard Carter, an English archeologist, had worked in Egypt for many years and had seen objects with the name of pharaoh Tutankhamun on them. No one knew where this king's tomb was, and Carter set out to find it. In 1917 he began searching in the Valley of the Kings. He paid men and boys to clear away thousands of tons of limestone rubble in the hope of finding Tutankhamun's lost tomb. After five years of this backbreaking work, Carter had found nothing. Then, in 1922, Carter's workers started to clear rubble from below the tomb of Ramesses VI—the very last place to look in the valley.

In November that year, Carter's luck changed. As the rubble was cleared, a flight of twelve steps going down into the ground was found. At the foot of the steps was the door to a tomb, and on the door was the name Tutankhamun. On the other side was a short corridor, and at the end of that was another door. Carter made a hole through the second door. He pushed a candle into the darkness within, and saw the glint of gold. It was an awesome sight—the intact tomb of an ancient Egyptian pharaoh, lost for 3,300 years. Carter had dreamed of discovering Tutankhamun's tomb, but he never imagined finding anything as spectacular as this.

The Death Mask

Perhaps the most amazing object from Tutankhamun's tomb is the death mask, which was placed over the head and shoulders of the pharaoh's mummy. It was made from two thin sheets of gold beaten into shape, inlaid with blue glass and pieces of blue, red, white, and black stones. The mask shows the pharaoh wearing a headcloth falling over his shoulders, and with a royal vulture and cobra on his forehead and a false beard on his chin.

▼ Tutankhamun's mummy still lies in its innermost coffin inside his tomb, where it was laid to rest 3,300 years ago.

FACT FILE

There were so many precious objects inside the tomb that it took Carter's team an incredible 10 years to carefully pack and remove them all.

LOST:
MACEDONIAN KING

The ancient Greeks regarded the nearby kingdom of Macedon as a backward region, which lay beyond their civilized world. However, when Philip II became king of Macedon, everything changed.

Location: Vergina, Greece
Date: about 336 BCE

Philip turned the Macedonian army into a formidable fighting force, and set about conquering cities in the north of Greece. One by one, Greek cities fell to him. Finally Athens, the main city, surrendered. Philip had conquered Greece, and Macedon had become the leading Greek state. Next, Philip began to make plans to defeat the Persians, who were the age-old enemies of the Greeks. But before he could carry out his plans, Philip was **assassinated** by one of his own bodyguards at his daughter's wedding.

▲ This carving of Philip was placed in his tomb. It shows a scar above his right eye, and Philip is known to have been injured by an arrow in that eye.

◀ A servant places a gold casket, containing the cremated bones of King Philip, inside a plain marble sarcophagus.

Royal Cemetery

Philip's burial mound was in a cemetery alongside more than 300 other burial mounds. Most were small, and had been built over the graves of ordinary people. Inside the larger mounds were the tombs belonging to Philip and other members of the Macedonian royal family. They were made of stone, with doors of solid marble and columns on the outside. Inside the tombs, the walls were plastered over and painted with pictures.

Philip's body was cremated and his burned bones were placed inside a gold box. Royal servants gathered together the box, the king's armor, silver cups and dishes, wreaths of golden leaves, and furniture. They placed these things inside a simple tomb: two rooms made from blocks of stone, built under the ground. They closed the tomb's outer door, and heaped a large mound of earth over it, creating a burial mound known as a **tumulus**.

◄ This golden quiver, a container for arrows, was placed inside Philip's tomb. It is decorated with battle scenes showing the capture of a city.

FOUND:

KING PHILIP II's TOMB

FACT FILE

Philip II was the father of Alexander the Great. Alexander completed his father's work by conquering the Persian empire.

The cemetery at Vergina, northern Greece, was well known to local people and to archeologists. One mound stood out more than all the others because it was the largest. It was known as the Great Tumulus, and in 1976 an excavation to uncover its secret began.

The excavation was led by Manolis Andronicos, a Greek archeologist. From the start, Andronicos felt sure he would find the tomb of a Macedonian king, as no one else would have had such a huge burial mound built in their honor. It was 360 feet (110 meters) in diameter, and 39 feet (12 meters) high, and would have been higher still when new.

▶ As the burial mound was cleared, Philip's tomb emerged from the earth. This shows the front of the tomb, with the entrance doorway still partly buried.

By August 1977, Andronicos had dug through the mound and was at ground level. He continued to dig, and when he found buried walls he knew he had discovered a tomb. A block of stone was lifted off the roof of the tomb, and a ladder was lowered inside. Andronicos climbed down, and as he gazed around he saw silver, bronze, and iron objects, and the twinkle of gold. Against a wall was a marble sarcophagus, and inside was a gold box which contained the burned, broken bones of a person. But whose were they?

The mystery was solved when Andronicos found a tiny ivory carving of a man's head. The sculptor had carved a scar above the man's right eye. For Andronicos, it was proof that he had found the tomb of King Philip II, who was known to have been blinded in his right eye by an arrow wound.

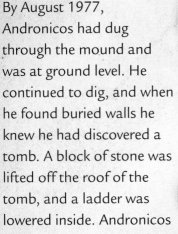

▲ This gold box, with the royal star of Macedon on its lid, contained the cremated bones of King Philip II.

The Face of Philip

Even though Philip's body had been cremated, his bones had not been burned to ashes. The fire had reduced them to small pieces, and it was possible for experts to rebuild his skeleton. His skull was pieced together, and a deep notch was found in the bone just above his right eye. This was an injury caused by an arrow. A medical artist used the skull to make a model of how Philip may have looked with his injured eye.

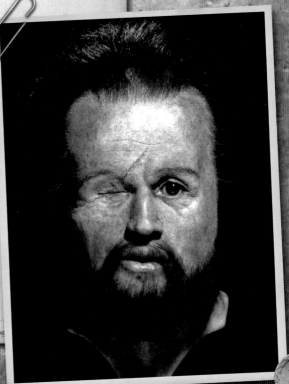

LOST:
SOUTH AMERICAN LORD

Long ago, Peru was home to the Moche people. The Moche buried their dead inside massive burial mounds that looked like flat-topped pyramids. They made these mounds from millions of mud bricks.

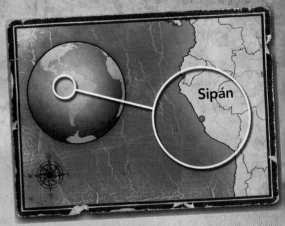

Location: Sipán, Peru
Date: about CE 700s

Long ago, a Moche ruler died. Because his real name is not known, he is referred to as the Lord of Sipán, after the place in northern Peru where he was buried. He may have been a warrior, a priest, or both. He was certainly important enough to be given a spectacular tomb.

The Lord of Sipán's body was buried with all sorts of precious objects, such as gold and copper headdresses and fans made of feathers. Servants wrapped his body and all these grave goods in three layers of colorful cloth, making a large bundle which fitted snugly inside a big wooden coffin. They lowered the coffin into a burial chamber, which was dug deep into the center of a mud brick pyramid.

◀ The Lord of Sipán, dressed in his royal regalia, stands with two attendants. Among the many ornaments he wears is a necklace of gold and silver beads in the shape of peanuts, a staple food of the Moche people.

▲ The Moche made beautiful objects from clay, such as these bottles in the shape of fierce jaguars. Liquid was poured from their mouths.

The Lord of Sipán did not go to his grave alone. Three men and two women were buried with him. They were sacrifices—people who had served him when he was alive, and who were killed so they could continue to work for him in the life after death. Workers sealed the chamber, then stacked layers of mud bricks above it.

Mud Brick Pyramids

When they were new, the Moche burial mounds had flat tops. These served as platforms, where temples were built and ceremonies performed. People walked up long, sloping ramps to reach the platforms. The whole structure was made of mud bricks, which were bricks of mud baked hard by the sun. Mud bricks could be made quickly and they were easy to build with, but they were easily worn away by rain and wind, and had to be replaced often.

FOUND:
LORD OF SIPÁN'S TOMB

By the 1980s, the ancient burial mounds at Sipán, Peru, had been worn away by centuries of rain and wind. The mud bricks had weathered into deep ruts and holes, and all trace of the mounds' flat tops and smooth sides had vanished.

Sipán's mounds became the target of tomb robbers, who dug into them looking for items to steal and sell. In 1987, the police found out what was happening at Sipán, and raided the looters' homes. They recovered a haul of treasure, and they called in a Peruvian archeologist, Walter Alva, to take a look. Alva could hardly believe his eyes. In front of him were gold objects of the highest quality, and he wondered what else might be inside the mounds at Sipán.

When Alva reached the site he saw that gold fever had gripped local villagers. They were digging into one of the Sipán mounds and destroying it. The police set up patrols to keep the villagers away so that Alva could begin his work. He knew the mound probably contained many tombs and the looters had found just one. Alva spotted a place the robbers had missed, and as he dug away the crumbled remains he revealed the outline of a coffin, untouched by the tomb robbers. Nothing had ever been found like it before. Alva named the dead man the Lord of Sipán, and his tomb is the richest ever found in South America.

▲ Deep inside the shaft dug by tomb robbers, archeologists begin the work of uncovering the tomb of the Lord of Sipán.

▶ The Lord of Sipán lies in the center, surrounded by four servants—women at his head and feet, men at his sides. A fifth servant, a man, was buried above the burial chamber, as if to guard it.

FACT FILE

As well as his servants, the Lord of Sipán's tomb also contained the body of a dog. It was probably his favorite pet.

Gold Pectoral

The Lord of Sipán was buried with eleven gold pectorals, or chest ornaments, on his body. They were probably part of his royal regalia, the ceremonial clothes and jewelry that he would have worn. This one was made in the shape of an octopus with a human head.

LOST:

ANGLO-SAXON KING

England was once divided into several kingdoms, and each of them was ruled by a powerful king. The eastern part of the country belonged to the **kingdom** of the East Angles, whose first king was Redwald. He was a **warrior king** who lived about 1,400 years ago.

Location: near Woodbridge, England
Date: about CE 625

The East Angles gave their name to an area of eastern England now known as East Anglia. They came to England from northern Germany, and by the 600s they had created one of the strongest kingdoms in the country. **Settlers** from other parts of Germany and northern Europe, such as the Saxons, formed their own kingdoms in England. Together, they are known as Anglo-Saxon kingdoms.

▶ The king was buried with a helmet with a **visor**, or face mask. It was found in pieces, and parts had rotted away. This reconstruction was made with the real pieces and some new parts to show how it may have looked.

Anglo-Saxon Swords

Swords were the main hand-to-hand weapons for Saxon warriors. They had iron blades, sharpened along both edges. The finest swords had gold ornaments decorated with red garnets (semiprecious stones). After a battle, the victors stripped the ornaments from the swords of defeated warriors. This was a way of showing total victory over an enemy. Warriors who died peacefully were often buried with their swords.

▼ Experts think that the body of King Redwald, and the grave goods buried with him, were placed in the center of the ship inside a wooden chamber.

The kingdoms fought one another and raided each other's territory. In one battle, fought in CE 616, King Redwald defeated the rival king of Northumbria. About nine years later King Redwald died. As a great warrior and king, he would have been laid to rest in a tomb built specially for him. It is likely that he was buried in a wooden ship dragged up onto the land, as were other rulers of the time from northern Europe. Everything a warrior king might need in the next life—his sword and helmet, his royal regalia (ceremonial items fit for a king), jewelry, fine clothes, and drinking horns for feasting—would have been placed around his body. Then, servants would have covered the ship in a huge mound of earth, and Redwald would have been left to travel on the long voyage into the afterlife.

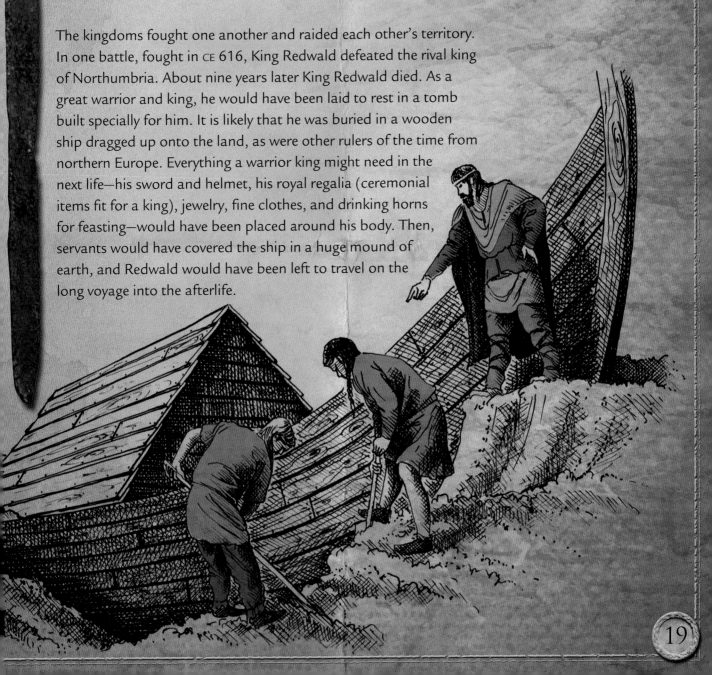

FOUND:

KING REDWALD'S TOMB?

In 1938, Edith Pretty decided to take a closer look at some mysterious mounds on her land at Sutton Hoo House, near the small town of Woodbridge in the east of England. She was interested in archeology, and wanted to know what, if anything, was inside them.

Edith Pretty contacted Basil Brown, a local archeologist. He began to excavate the mounds. There were several small mounds, and one that was much bigger than the rest. Brown dug into three of the small mounds and identified them as Anglo-Saxon burial mounds. Tomb robbers had raided them long before. There was little to be found, apart from some big iron nails of the type used to hold wooden planks together on Anglo-Saxon ships.

Later, Brown dug into the big mound. Again, he found ship's nails. As he removed more of the sandy soil, he saw the nails were in rows. Slowly, the ghostly impression of an ancient **longboat** was revealed. The wood had disappeared, but the rows of nails showed where the planks had once been. In the center of the ship was a burial chamber, untouched by any tomb robbers. The contents were stunning: weapons and armor, coins and jewelry, silver and bronze bowls, and many other fine objects. All that was missing was a body, which the acid soil had dissolved, bones and all. It is impossible for experts to be certain who was buried in the Sutton Hoo ship. But the person was clearly important, and many believe the ship was the burial place of Redwald, king of the East Angles.

► This solid gold belt buckle from Sutton Hoo would have been owned by a very wealthy man—perhaps King Redwald himself.

▼ This small bronze plaque would have been fixed to the side of a large pitcher. It is decorated with a pattern made from colorful enamel.

▲ The ghostly outline of the Anglo-Saxon ship. The original wood had rotted away, and the archeologists found only impressions left in the sand, plus hundreds of iron nails that had once joined the planks together.

Sutton Hoo Burial Ground

There are about 20 burial mounds at Sutton Hoo, probably all the graves of important people. But Sutton Hoo was also the burial place of people who died violently, either from hanging or beheading. They were buried in ordinary graves near the burial mounds. Experts do not know whether these are the graves of criminals executed for their crimes, or of people sacrificed when an important person was buried.

LOST:
HAN PRINCE

Ancient China was divided up into different states, which were ruled by powerful families, or **dynasties**. One of the strongest was the Han Dynasty, which controlled a large area in the east of China about 2,000 years ago.

Location: Lingshan, Mancheng County, southwest China
Date: 113 BCE

The Han Dynasty lasted for about 400 years, and during that time China prospered. The population increased, farmers cultivated more land, and arts and crafts flourished. Many new things were invented, including paper, miniature hot-air balloons, and the wheelbarrow. A major trade route was set up, linking China with people far to the west. The Silk Route, as it came to be known, stretched across the vast continent of Asia to the shores of the Mediterranean Sea—a distance of 1,550 miles (2,500 kilometers).

◄ This painting shows the Han Dynasty army on the move. The Han government conquered and settled new lands, expanding its territories.

The Magic of Jade

Jade is a hard, smooth stone, usually green or white. It has always been highly valued in China, more than silver or gold, because people believed it had magical powers. They thought jade could protect the dead, and stop the body from rotting away. Ancient Chinese emperors and nobles wore pieces of carved jade, and jade objects were buried with them in their tombs.

In 113 BCE, Prince Liu Sheng, the son of the emperor of China, died. A tomb was built for the prince inside a mountain. A long passageway was dug into it and, at the end, a large room was carved out of the solid rock. The tomb was filled with 2,700 grave goods for Liu Sheng to use in the afterlife. There were chariots, silks, and items made of precious jade, gold, and silver. Lamps were placed around the tomb to light up the darkness of the underground burial chamber.

But most stunning of all was the prince's body. He was dressed from head to foot in a suit made from almost 2,500 pieces of green jade, sewn together with gold wire. This incredible jade suit was designed to protect Liu Sheng's body forever.

▼ Objects for Prince Liu Sheng to use in the afterlife filled the passageway that led to his burial chamber inside the mountain.

FOUND:

LIU SHENG'S TOMB

The mountain at Lingshan, in southwest China, kept its secret well. For more than 2,000 years, Prince Liu Sheng's secret resting place was safe. Tomb robbers never raided it, and earthquakes never damaged it.

Then, in 1968, soldiers from the Chinese army climbed the mountain. They found what they thought was a cave, and went inside. The soldiers soon came across bronze, jade, and pottery objects. They seemed very old, so the soldiers told the authorities. A team of archeologists was called in, and very soon they realized the soldiers had stumbled across a huge tomb dug deep into the mountain.

The tomb had several rooms. On either side of the entrance passage were two store rooms. One was crammed with chariots and horses' skeletons. The other room contained cooking utensils, tableware and jars for wine, grain, fish, and meat. At the end of the passageway was a large room whose walls had once been lined with wood.

▶ Lady Dou Wan, the wife of Prince Liu Sheng, was buried in a tomb next to her husband's, also found in 1968. Dou Wan's body was also dressed in a suit made from pieces of jade joined together with gold wire.

The room was filled with bronze objects and figures of servants. A marble door led into a smaller room, and inside was a heap of jade squares. The squares seemed to be arranged in the shape of a human body. Inscriptions on grave goods revealed that this was the tomb of Prince Liu Sheng. His body had rotted away, and his jade burial suit had slowly collapsed. The suit was taken to a museum where it was put back together, until it seemed as if Prince Liu Sheng was inside it once more.

Incense

Prince Liu Sheng was buried with this incense burner, made in the shape of a mountain. As the incense burned, sweet-smelling smoke rose out of holes in the container, like mist covering a mountain. Incense was burned to please the gods, who were thought to like its smell.

FACT FILE

Many archeologists believed that jade burial suits were a myth until those of Prince Liu Sheng and Lady Dou Wan were discovered.

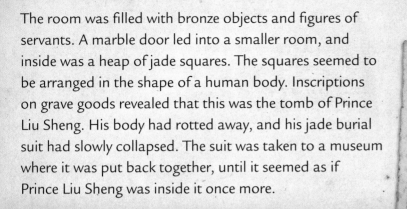

◀ The jade suit inside which Prince Liu Sheng was buried may have taken 10 years to make. It would have been started while he was alive.

LOST: KINGS AND QUEENS OF UR

About 4,500 years ago, a great city of 20,000 people flourished in the south of Iraq. Its name was Ur. The city was ruled over by a powerful king. He was chief priest, head of the army, and leader of the government.

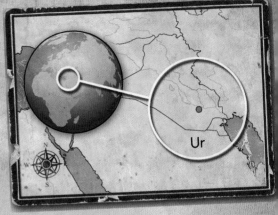

Location: Ur, modern-day Iraq
Date: 2500 BCE

When the king died, he was laid to rest in a cemetery alongside the tombs of those kings who had ruled before him. Each tomb was an underground chamber made from brick and stone. A steep ramp sloped down to the **burial chamber** from the surface, and on the day a king was buried, his body was carried down the ramp. He was laid on a wooden platform inside the chamber, and grave goods were placed around his body.

▼ In the city center of Ur stood a high tower called a **ziggurat**. It was a holy building and the center of religious life in the city. Its platforms were reached by ramps and staircases. At the very top was a temple to the moon god, Nanna.

Priest Kings

In ancient Mesopotamia, where the present-day countries of Iraq and Iran are, the king was believed to be the representative of the gods on Earth. In this stone panel from the city of Ur, King Ur-Nammu is shown as a priest, making an offering to the moon god Nanna (the seated figure). It was during King Ur-Nammu's reign that the ziggurat of Ur was built.

The dead king was given everything he would need in the next life. Chariots, weapons, armor, jewelry, musical instruments, and many other objects were buried with him. But the king needed more than this. He needed people to serve him in his new life after death. So, into the burial chamber went the king's servants—bodyguards, musicians, and ladies in waiting. Each person carried a cup of poison. They were prepared to die for their dead king, because they believed they would continue to serve him in the afterlife. When the last of these human sacrifices had died, workers filled the tomb with earth, and the dead were left to rest in peace.

▼ Holding cups of poison, 74 men and women took their final steps down into the burial chamber. It is likely that being chosen to be sacrificed with the dead king was a great honor.

27

FOUND:

ROYAL CEMETERY OF UR

In the 1920s, archeologists began to excavate an ancient mound in the south of Iraq, which local people called Tell al-Muqayyar. The archeologists knew it was the city of Ur, and they were determined to uncover its buried secrets.

An English archeologist named Leonard Woolley led the excavations. As he dug into the mound, he began to uncover the remains of Ur's ancient buildings. He revealed the city's ziggurat, the houses of the people who once lived there, and the places where they worked. Then, beneath a thick layer of silt, Woolley found a cemetery where more than 2,500 people were buried. These were the very people who had worshipped at the temple on top of the ziggurat, some 4,500 years ago. However, it was not the simple graves of these ordinary people that made headlines around the world.

▼ The ruins of Ur, with the great ziggurat towering over the city.

In the same cemetery, Woolley found the tombs of 16 important people. Although some of the tombs had been broken into long before, Woolley found others that the looters had missed. He believed he had found the tombs of Ur's kings and queens. He uncovered precious objects bearing their names, such as King Meskalamdug and Queen Pu-abi. But, when more human skeletons were discovered, Woolley realized he was looking at the remains of human sacrifices. Woolley felt sure that these people had died willingly, because there were no signs of violence or struggle on the bones.

▶ A gold head dress adorns the skull of a long-dead queen of Ur. Around her neck is a bead and gold necklace.

The King's Helmet

King Meskalamdug was buried with a gold helmet bearing his name. It was made from a single thin sheet of gold, beaten into shape. The helmet was decorated with a pattern that looked like wavy hair, to make it look as if the king was wearing a golden wig.

TIMELINE
OF DISCOVERIES

1800s
Hundreds of ancient tombs are found in Etruria, Italy. They belong to the Etruscan civilization, which existed in Italy before the Romans.

1876
German archeologist Heinrich Schliemann finds the rich graves of people who ruled Mycenae, an ancient city in Greece.

1922
British archeologist Howard Carter discovers the tomb of pharaoh Tutankhamun in the Valley of the Kings, Egypt.

1920s
The tombs of kings and queens who ruled the ancient city of Ur are found in Iraq by British archeologist Leonard Woolley.

1939
The tomb of an important Anglo-Saxon, possibly King Redwald, is found at Sutton Hoo, England.

1968
The tombs of Prince Liu Sheng and his wife Dou Wan are found at Lingshan, China. The royal couple is dressed in suits made from hundreds of pieces of jade.

1977
The tomb of the Marquis Yi, an important noble, is found in central China. Inside are hundreds of objects, including many musical instruments and weapons.

1977
The tomb of King Philip II of Macedon is found at Vergina, Greece. He was the father of Alexander the Great.

1987
The tomb of the Lord of Sipán is found by tomb robbers at Sipán, Peru. It is later excavated by archeologists.

1995
Tomb KV5 in the Valley of the Kings, Egypt, is extensively explored by archeologists for the first time. They find underground corridors and more than 70 rooms, which makes it the largest tomb in the valley.

2011
A tomb found near Jerusalem, Israel, is claimed to be that of Zechariah, an ancient Hebrew prophet.

GLOSSARY

archeologist
A person who digs up and studies the remains of the past.

assassinate
To kill an important person by violent means.

BCE
Used in dates to mean "Before the Common Era." The Common Era begins with year 1.

burial chamber
A room where a dead person is buried. It is usually specially made for this purpose.

CE
Used in dates to mean "Common Era." The Common Era begins with year 1, which is the same as the year AD 1 in the Christian calendar.

dynasty
A series of powerful families, such as the ancient Chinese rulers or the ancient Egyptian pharaohs.

kingdom
A place ruled by a king.

long boat
A long, narrow boat with a sail and oars. Also called longship.

mummified
Describes the body of a dead person or animal which has been preserved to keep it from rotting away.

pharaoh
A king or a queen of Ancient Egypt.

sacrifice
Killing an animal or a person to please a god.

sarcophagus
A coffin made from stone.

settlers
People who travel to new places to start new lives, away from their own lands.

shrine
A holy place dedicated to a particular god, and used for worship.

tomb robber
A person who looks for tombs, breaks into them, and steals their contents.

treasure hunter
A person who searches for treasure. Some treasure hunters damage ancient sites and break the law in their search. Others work with archeologists.

tumulus
A hill made of earth built over the burial place of a dead person.

visor
The front part of a helmet, covering the face.

warrior king
A ruler who was also a fighter who led his army in battle.

ziggurat
A stepped pyramid, composed of flat platforms and with a temple on the top.

INDEX